5 SECONDS OF SUMMER

LIVE AND LOUD

THIS IS A CARLTON BOOK

Copyright © 2015 Carlton Books Limited

First published in 2015 by Carlton Books Limited,
a division of the Carlton Publishing Group,
20 Mortimer Street, London W1T 3JW

10 9 8 7 6 5 4 3 2 1

A CIP catalogue for this book is available from the
British Library.

ISBN: 978-1-78097-725-6

Printed in China

PLEASE NOTE: This book is not affiliated with or
endorsed by 5 Seconds of Summer or any of their
publishers or licensees.

5 SECONDS OF SUMMER

LIVE AND LOUD

The Ultimate
On-tour Fanbook

CARLTON
BOOKS

"IT'S CRAZY FOR US, BUT WE'RE SO GRATEFUL FOR EVERY SINGLE PERSON THAT SUPPORTS US, NOT MANY PEOPLE WHERE WE LIVE GET THIS KIND OF OPPORTUNITY TO DO WHAT THEY LOVE," -CALUM

CONTENTS

ROCKING THE 2014 *BILLBOARD* MUSIC AWARDS, MAY 18, 2014 IN LAS VEGAS. SPOT THE UNDERPANTS ABOVE MICHAEL'S HEAD!

A BACKSTAGE BROMANCE BLOSSOMS BETWEEN THE BOYS BEFORE THE 2014 AMERICAN MUSIC AWARDS IN LOS ANGELES!

LIVE AND LOUD

5 SECONDS OF SUMMER, OR 5SOS AS THEY ARE KNOWN TO THEIR MILLIONS OF ADORING FANS, MAY HAVE HAD A NUMBER 1 ALBUM AND SOLD OUT STADIUMS WORLDWIDE, BUT—AS THE BOYS THEMSELVES WOULD AGREE—WHEN IT COMES TO GETTING UP CLOSE AND PERSONAL WITH THE BAND, NOTHING ON EARTH BEATS SEEING THEM LIVE AND LOUD ONSTAGE.

Ever since the band played their first gig on December 3, 2011 at The Annandale Hotel in Western Sydney, the Australian pop-punk and rock quartet of Mike, Ash, Cal, and Luke have had one vision: "It was a dream of ours to be up on a stage playing our own original music and to have crowds sing our songs back at us!" said Mike in 2014. That dream has now come true—and better than the boys could ever have imagined!

For the past four years, 5SOS has been selling out headline tours in Australia, the U.S., Europe, the U.K., and—as of February 2015—Asia, supporting the world's biggest band of the twenty-first century, One Direction—all before they'd even released a first single of their own! This is a band that can do the impossible, achieve the magical, and rock out with their socks out until every screaming fan at one of their shows is exhausted from jumping around too much!

After the release of their million-selling single "She Looks So Perfect" in February 2014—a song that saw an unexpected 10 percent surge in sales of American Apparel underwear, thanks to their quirky lyrics—the band has entered the arena as one of the planet's most exciting new bands. And this incredible success means they are always on the road. "I think the best thing about our fans is that they are from all over the place so we don't stay in one place for very long!" said Ashton in 2015, as they embarked on their first worldwide headline tour in support of their multi-platinum debut album, 5 Seconds of Summer. It's a tour that will see them play more than 70 shows in six months to almost a million fans!

And this is just the beginning. 5SOS are here to stay, but they don't stick around in one place for long. So, if they come to a city near you... make sure you have your tickets booked, your bandanas on, and you're ready to rock! Because when 5SOS come to town, it's a live experience like no other!

LUKE LIKES TO GET AS CLOSE TO HIS FANS AS POSSIBLE DURING THE *PEOPLE* MAGAZINE AWARDS IN LOS ANGELES!

BREAKING THE INTERNET

ON DECEMBER 3, 2011, MIKE, CAL, LUKE, AND AHSTON PLAYED THEIR FIRST EVER GIG. TWELVE PEOPLE SHOWED UP. ON JUNE 14, 2015, 5SOS PLAYED THE HISTORIC SSE ARENA IN LONDON. TWELVE THOUSAND FANS SHOWED UP! LET'S GET THE PARTY STARTED!

ATTENDING THE 2014 MTV VIDEO MUSIC AWARDS, THE BOYS PERFORMED "AMNESIA." THE MUSIC VIDEO NOW HAS MORE THAN 60 MILLION YOUTUBE VIEWS!

Five Seconds of Summer are a phenomenon. In four short years they have gone from being four teenage boys rehearsing in their parents' garages in Sydney, Australia, to becoming one of the biggest, loudest, and best pop-rock-punk bands, with millions of fans all over the world, a Number 1 debut album that has sold three million copies, and more than five million single sales so far. But the big numbers don't stop there. Since 2011, the band has performed at a variety of radio shows, award ceremonies, and TV appearances, and has played hundreds of gigs at several of the world's largest arenas and international stadiums with the greatest boy band of all time, One Direction. How on earth did they do all this... before they had even reached the age of 18? It's a fair question, and one that even the boys cannot answer.

"I'm not sure we've taken over the world yet... but we're working on it!" Luke declared. "The band became the four piece it is now on December 4, 2011," the singer continued, "and none of us ever imagined that we would be in another country on the other side of the planet recording our first ever album a year later!" he remarked in 2012.

But let's not get ahead of ourselves just yet. Let's rewind. Before the fame and worldwide tours—before 5 Seconds of Summer had even been shortened to 5SOS—they were just three boys who knew each other from various classes while attending their secondary school, Norwest Christian College in Sydney, Australia. The trio of

Mike, Cal, and Luke began rehearsing after school, but they couldn't think of a name. Originally they wanted to call the group Bromance because they all felt a special brotherly connection when they first started jamming and wanted a name to reflect that chemistry. As Calum remembers about their unique bro-show at the time, "The three of us went to the same school in New South Wales in Sydney—Michael, Luke, and I—and in 9th grade Luke started posting some covers just by himself on acoustic guitar, and Michael was like, 'Hey man, do you wanna start a band?' and Luke was like, 'OK,' and I think I just kind of wedged myself in there somehow! We were just messing around on YouTube putting up covers. We booked a gig at some pub [The Annandale Hotel] and we needed a drummer, since we booked it without having a drummer. Michael sent a Facebook message to Ashton, who he knew through one of our friends, and was like, 'Hey man, there's gonna be so many people at this gig we just booked. How would you like to come drum with us?' and Ashton was like, 'Hell yeah, that sounds sick!,' and then 12 people showed up and it was the worst gig that had ever happened! It was my first time ever playing on a bass, because I played guitar but I was forced to play bass because I was the least good on guitar."

The band laughs about this first gig now, especially after realizing immediately that their "bromance" was something special, a kindred meeting of spirits that they could all feel right away. "When we met, we realized we're the same. We knew we didn't necessarily belong," Ash said highlighting that their tiny community where they grew up didn't always appreciate teenage boys playing loud punk rock, who didn't necessarily fit in. Luke agrees: "It's been incredible for a rock-pop band like us to come from such a small school in a small town and to be able to do what we do."

After a few gigs, and a "little following" (to quote Cal) thanks to the YouTube sessions, the quartet were on their way to becoming local celebrities, well, sort of! But before they began performing their own original music, the boys posted covers of Blink-182 and Mayday Parade songs—sometimes using two acoustic guitars, with Ash on the bongos. The video that took off was their unplugged version of a song by R&B artist Chris Brown (ft. Justin Bieber): "Next 2 You,"

which has earned 2.5 million YouTube views since being posted in July 2011. You should check out some of the comments—hilarious!

"We were building a fan base, but we sort of wanted to be like a live band known for our live performances," said Ashton, talking about the band's early live gigs. "That was the biggest job, transferring a YouTube audience to people who will actually come down to our show." But Ash had no need to worry. As it happened, a certain Louis Tomlinson had seen the boys' YouTube clips and tweeted about them. "Louis found us on YouTube and was like, 'We should do something with this band,' said Calum. "It's crazy... because nothing really happens to bands from Western Sydney."

Louis and the rest of the One Direction boys may be 5SOS's shining stars and mentors, but the band's success, following Louis' mega-tweet, is all down to a winning combination of hard work, a sprinkle of luck, and sweat from thousands of performances to hone their live show into an unforgettable experience!

5SOS ON YOUTUBE!

These are some of 5SOS's earliest YouTube clips. Check them out!

1_Luke performs "A Drop in the Ocean" by Ron Pope.

2_Mike and Luke, very cute, sing Justin Bieber!

3_Cal, Mike, Luke, and Ash play "Teenage Dirtbag" with acoustic guitars.

4_Cal and Luke cover Ed Sheeran's "The A Team."

5_Mike, Luke, and Cal perform "Next 2 You."

THE GUYS GO GREEN ONSTAGE AT NICKELODEON'S 28TH ANNUAL KIDS' CHOICE AWARDS, LOS ANGELES, MARCH 28, 2015. THE PHOTOS AND VIDEOS OF THE BAND GETTING SLIMED BECAME A VIRAL SENSATION ONLINE.

THE GUYS RECEIVE THE AWARD FOR "SONG OF THE YEAR" DURING THE ARIA AWARDS IN SYDNEY! THEIR MOMS WERE PROUD!

5 SECONDS OF SUMMER PLAYLIST

WHAT'S YOUR FAVORITE SONG?

"She Looks So Perfect"
"Don't Stop"
"Good Girls"
"Kiss Me Kiss Me"
"18"
"Everything I Didn't Say"
"Beside You"-Mike's fave song
to play live!
"End up Here"
"Long Way Home"
"Heartbreak Girl"
"English Love Affair"
"Amnesia"

PROJECTED ONTO THE SIDE OF A TALL LONDON BUILDING, THE BAND CELEBRATE THEIR DEBUT ALBUM IN SUPER COOL STYLE.

NUMBER ONE AND ONLY

ON JUNE 27, 2014—AFTER THREE YEARS OF MAKING THEIR FANS WAIT!—5SOS FINALLY RELEASED THEIR DEBUT ALBUM, *5 SECONDS OF SUMMER*. IT WENT TO NUMBER 1 IN MORE THAN TEN COUNTRIES! WITH THE TITLE OF THE ALBUM BEING JUST THE BAND'S NAME, THEIR INTENTION FOR THE RECORD WAS MADE LOUD AND CLEAR: THEY ARE PROUD TO BE WHO THEY ARE!

It wasn't just details of their debut album that the band made public in the summer of 2014. The cool quartet also announced the news of their Hi or Hey record label (named after a quote from one of their first ever interviews). The announcement of this label stunned the music industry and journalists: It was the first time that a rebel band of teenage musicians had set up their own label—before they had even released their own debut album! All of the band's music will be released on Hi or Hey Records from now on.

In order to become the live band they wanted to be, and in order to sound as accomplished as possible, just as their heroes Green Day, Nirvana, and Blink-182 had done before them—Nirvana famously ditched whole songs in the studio if they couldn't nail them in one take!—5SOS started doing some loopy things in the studio too.

"We rehearsed in the dark!" Luke revealed. "We thought if we can't see what we are doing, and we can still play, then we might sound good when the lights are turned on. We wanted to be a credible live band so people would come and see us and say 'That's better than what we hear on the record.'" And, judging by fan comments so far, this crazy idea has paid off. In a short space of time, the guys have gone from being garage-band noise-monsters to accomplished and professional-sounding musicians who know how to grab the audience's attention, both on record and playing live. It's so fascinating that people say, 'They can really play,'" Luke has stated. "We didn't know it was meant to be a weird thing that we could actually play instruments and write music."

All 12 tracks on *5 Seconds of Summer* are written by the boys, but early on the group decided that they would split into pairs and write separately, which is why many of the tracks on the album are written by either Ash and Mike, such as "She Looks So Perfect," or by Calum and Luke, such as "Don't Stop." "The only way to be original in your songwriting is to write about your own experiences, and I think that's what we try to do as a band," Luke declared. The gang has said for the next album that they will all write together, they will all write separately, and as with the first album, they will work with other songwriters too. In January 2015, the band was seen in the studio composing new material with Benji and Joel Madden from Good Charlotte —hopefully due for release at the end of 2015! "We've discovered our sound now," Calum said after finishing the record. "I'm really excited to write the next album. We have so many ideas, and I'm really ready to mature our sound, definitely make it a more organic sound, just drum, bass, and two guitars."

Upon its mouth-watering release, *5 Seconds of Summer* became the highest-selling debut album in eight years in the US, selling 259,000 copies in its first week, and made them the first Australian act to debut at Number 1 with their first full-length album! A mighty achievement. To celebrate their arrival into the world as fully fledged popstars, Ashton tweeted, "To everyone that's been a part of the journey so far we love you so much, you guys made the album number #1 in the US, we are speechless..." Michael hilariously tweeted: "Literally CANNOT believe we can say we had a number 1 album in the US... WE FINALLY BEAT FROZEN." Typical Mike!

THE ONLY WAY IS UP!

IF IT WASN'T FOR ONE DIRECTION, 5 SECONDS OF SUMMER MAY NOT HAVE HAD THE CHANCE TO MAKE IT BIG OUTSIDE OF THEIR HOMELAND, AUSTRALIA, NO MATTER HOW HARD THEY TRIED. BUT FATE STEPPED IN AND NOW ONE DIRECTION AND 5SOS ARE THE BEST OF FRIENDS AND PLANET-DEVOURING PERFORMING PARTNERS. SURELY THE TIME HAS COME FOR BOTH BANDS TO JOIN FORCES AND BECOME ONE BIG SUPERGROUP? WHAT DO YOU THINK THEY COULD BE CALLED—5SOS1D, OR 51 DIRECTIONS OF SUMMER? "WHO KNOWS, IT COULD HAPPEN!" SAID MIKE. FINGERS CROSSED, EVERYONE!

One look at Niall Horan's Twitter account and you'll quickly realize the love between his band, One Direction, and 5SOS.

If you've ever been to a One Direction concert, you'll know that 5SOS performs for 45 minutes before One Direction does their thing. Quite often, 5SOS will jump onto the stage while One Direction is performing and pump up the audience even more, as well as prank Harry, Liam, Niall, Zayn (before his sad departure in March 2015), and Louis. On extra-special occasions the two bands perform together too, like when they all sang "Teenage Dirtbag" on the final night of the *Take Me Home Tour* in Australia, on October 30, 2013. The song ended in one massive pie fight onstage—check out the clip on YouTube; it's fan-tastic! Another fan favorite is the YouTube video of One Direction singing "She Looks So Perfect" to their fans! It's amazing—and sounds great!

Despite being labeled the "next One D" by the music press—a comparison that Ash feels is "kind of awkward"—the nine boys get along really well. It's one of the main reasons why 5SOS has been asked back to perform on all three of One Direction's major stadium tours, *Take Me Home* (2013), *Where We Are Now* (2014), and *On the Road Again* (2015).

"It's crazy to be on tour with the world's biggest band!" Ashton said, as they embarked on 2015's *On the Road Again Tour*. "Niall's got a good sense of humor and he loves rock bands. We really bond over that." It is Niall, the blond Irish One Directioner who plays guitar live, who is most impressed with his rockstar pals, often tweeting and posting the most number of 5SOSelfies, as they should be known!

Will the guys continue to tour with One Direction in the years to come? Who knows. But with 5SOS's own headline tours about to get bigger, better, and bolder... it wouldn't be a suprise if the quartet became too big to tour with their old pals. You never know, 5SOS could become so super-massive that even One Direction may become *their* support band. Imagine that—what a show it would be!

WANT TO SEE 1D AND 5SOS BEING ALL BROMANTIC TOGETHER?

CHECK OUT THESE YOUTUBE CLIPS!

1_One Direction and 5SOS "Teenage Dirtbag" Pie Fight onstage!

2_5SOS prank 1D during "Kiss" onstage wearing 1D face masks!

3_Louis and Zayn perform "Heartbreak Girl" at a gig in Manchester!

SUPPORTING ONE DIRECTION ON THEIR *WHERE WE ARE TOUR* IN GERMANY, JULY 2014. WERE YOU THERE?

"THEY ARE REALLY SWEET GUYS AND THEY SUPPORT US SO MUCH AND HOPEFULLY THEY LET US SUPPORT THEM BACK. WE HAVE NOTHING BUT GOOD THINGS TO SAY ABOUT THEM, THEY ARE SO HARD-WORKING."
-ASHTON, ON 1D

5SOS-MANIA!

5SOS FANS ARE THE BEST IN THE WORLD. IT'S OFFICIAL. THEY HAVE SUPPORTED AND CELEBRATED THE BAND FROM THEIR EARLY YOUTUBE DAYS, RIGHT THROUGH TO TRAVELING ALL OVER THE WORLD TO SEE THEIR FAVORITE AUSSIE BOYS AT ONE OF THEIR OWN SHOWS-OFTEN LINING UP SEVERAL HOURS BEFORE THE GIG, JUST TO GET AS CLOSE AS THEY CAN TO THEIR HEROES. FROM THE U.S. TO EUROPE, JAPAN TO AUSTRALIA, THE "5SOS FAM" IS JUST AS LIVE AND LOUD AS 5SOS ITSELF!

5 Seconds of Summer are at their happiest when they are performing onstage to The Fam. It is their most cherished place in the world, especially when thousands of their fans are singing their own songs back to them and having a really good time. It's a dream come true for everyone.

"They're all loud, and they're all very excited!" Ashton has said about his millions of fans. He's a drummer who knows that in these days of social media, being connected with your fanbase 24 hours a day and being able to reach out and talk and share things with them is more important than anything else, and the band's Number 1 priority. "We're very open about who we are," Ashton declared in a recent interview. "It isn't the 1980s anymore, you can't be a mysterious dude and a huge rock star—people want real people. It's great that people even listen to your music, especially being a band that grew out of my mom's garage, and it's great that people pay attention to what we're doing and see us as a band that makes good music." This closeness, the special bond the band likes to have with their fans, extends to even perhaps being open to the idea of dating them? Mike has said that he would date a fan, if he feels like it could be a serious relationship: "Fans are the same thing as a normal person, but they just like your band. It's like a bonus!" Luke agreed: "I would date a fan. People talk about fans like they're mystical creatures, but they're just normal people."

Whether talking to fans lining up before a radio show, making a TV appearance, or being chased down the street by autograph-hunting (and selfie!) fans, 5SOS knows that in the twenty-first century a strong and direct relationship with their fans is important if they want to grow as artists and continue to make music that people want to hear. With more than five million Twitter followers each, 5SOS aren't short of fans—but don't expect any of the boys to get a big head... just yet! "We always say it's weird that fans want to meet us," Mike disclosed. "Even when we're in Milan or New York, fans will be hanging around the radio stations or wherever we are doing promo. When that happens, I always think 'Those fans are here to see us? But I'm not that special!'" Awww, how cute is Mike?

ASH AND HIS ICONIC BANDANA SAY HELLO TO SOME LUCKY FANS. THE BAND IS ALWAYS HAPPY TO TAKE 5SOSELFIES!

LUKE FACES THE CROWD DURING "DON'T STOP" AT THE 2014 IHEARTRADIO FESTIVAL, LAS VEGAS—A LONG WAY FROM HOME.

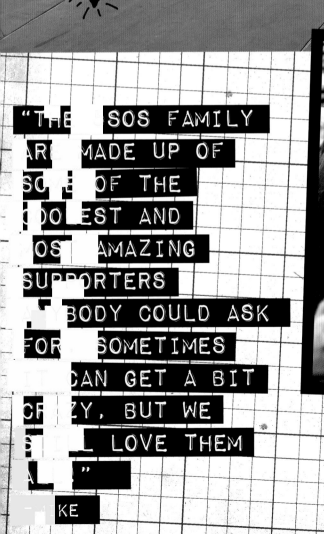

"THE SOS FAMILY ARE MADE UP OF SOME OF THE COOLEST AND MOST AMAZING SUPPORTERS ANYBODY COULD ASK FOR. SOMETIMES IT CAN GET A BIT CRAZY, BUT WE STILL LOVE THEM ALL."
— LUKE

LUKE TAKES A SILLY SELFIE WITH ONE LUCKY FAN WHO GOT TO MEET THE ENTIRE BAND—DREAMS DO COME TRUE!

ON THE ROAD

5SOS HAS BEEN CONSTANTLY OUT ON THE ROAD, USUALLY IN THEIR TOUR BUS, CALLED "GUS." FROM THEIR OPENING ACT SLOTS WITH HOT CHELLE RAE IN OCTOBER 2012, THROUGH TO THEIR OWN HEADLINE TOURS, THE BOYS ARE ALWAYS EN ROUTE TO A STAGE NEAR YOU. "I ABSOLUTELY LOVE BEING ON A TOUR BUS," ASHTON SAYS. "IT'S KINDA LIKE A LITTLE TIME CAPSULE..."

"I remember we were touring," explained Calum in 2012. "We were doing a headline tour around Australia and we were having lunch and we had this piece of paper that was put in front of us telling us we were doing a world tour and listing all the venues... and it was just endless pieces of paper. Mind-blowing!"

Ever since that day, 5SOS has been on a mind-blowing journey around the planet, and has played more than one hundred shows a year, to stadiums with a capacity of more than eighty thousand people! If you were to do the math of how many people 5SOS has played for—so far—you'd get a headache very quickly, but it would be close to two million!

In the summer of 2012, the band went on three tours, to support their debut single "Out of My Limit" as well as their *Unplugged* and *Somewhere New* EPs, which had received an increasing amount of radio and press attention. Despite being only one year old, and with no financial help from a record label, 5 Seconds of Summer deliberately increased their number of live performances to help boost their increasingly spectacular fan awareness—a key ingredient for a band who had become not only minor celebrities on social media, but in their home town, too. The boys never believed they were going to break into the big time, but they had the patience to keep on playing small shows, hone their sound, write loads of songs they loved playing live, and gel together as musicians and friends. "When you start a band, you kind of just do it for fun," Mike said. "You can never expect what's going to happen, so when success does happen, it's just amazing." As luck would have it, Louis from One Direction gave them a foot up and the band was suddenly thrown into the limelight! They were asked to join Niall, Harry,

Zayn, Liam, and Louis on their *Take Me Home Tour* 2013.

"We were on our own tour in Adelaide at the time," says Ashton, describing the moment when they first got the call that changed their lives. "We found out that Louis had found out about us on YouTube and we were like "WHOA." We were just a tiny, tiny band from Sydney and he tweeted about us... and then it all just blossomed from there very quickly. It took us a while to decide what we wanted to do and if it was the right thing to do... and it definitely was!" Ashton says of the historic moment. It was then that the group knew they had the opportunity to make all their dreams

come true. "Learning how to tour from the 1D lads really changed our lives," Calum revealed. "I still can't believe it happened!".

With the *Take Me Home Tour* in the bag with 1D, 5SOS went into the studio and recorded "Out of My Limit," which was released on November 19, 2012. The music video for the song received more than 100,000 views in the first 24 hours. Riding high on that success, the boys departed in December to London on a quest to write more hit songs with various artists including McFly, Roy Stride of Scouting For Girls, Nick Hodgson of Kaiser Chiefs, Jamie Scott, Jake Sinclair, Jake Gosling, Steve Robson, and James Bourne of McBusted. In May 2012, 5SOS announced

tour dates at Factory Theatre in Sydney, Old Museum in Brisbane, and Xavier College in Melbourne. All shows sold out within two minutes of going on sale and crashed the ticketing websites! Following the success of the June 2012 release of their *Unplugged* EP, the band embarked on their *Twenty Twelve Mini Australian Tour*, playing dates at Uni Bar in Adelaide, Oxford Art Factory in Sydney, Old Museum in Brisbane, and Corner Hotel in Melbourne. It wasn't until November 3, 2012, however, that 5SOS played their first (of many!) international headline show, while on a break from the One Direction tour. The band jumped on a plane and played to 250 fans at the Zeal Cafe, in Auckland, New Zealand.

"YOU FALL ASLEEP EVERY DAY AND THEN WAKE UP IN A NEW STATE OR COUNTRY, THAT'S PROBABLY THE BEST THING." LUKE LOVES TOURING THE WORLD ONBOARD THE "GUS BUS."

SOUND OF MUSIC

2013 WAS THE YEAR THAT 5SOS WENT FROM BEING FOUR BOYS WHO HAD ONLY JUST LEFT SCHOOL TO BECOMING PROFESSIONAL, FULL-TIME EMPLOYED MUSICIANS WHO HAD ALREADY CIRCLED THE GLOBE PERFORMING THEIR MUSIC TO PEOPLE ON NEARLY ALL THE CONTINENTS ON THE PLANET. WHAT ON EARTH WERE THEY GOING TO DO NEXT?

ASH MAY KEEP THE BEAT GOING AT THE BACK, BUT HE ALWAYS COMES OUT FROM THE DRUMS AT LEAST ONCE DURING A SHOW, OFTEN TO THROW HIS STICKS INTO THE CROWD!

2012 had seen the band expand their songwriting experience and develop their own sound, spending time in the studio with songwriters Christian Lo and Joel Chapman of Amy Meredith. The year 2013 saw them on the road from February to November, on One Direction's staggering *Take Me Home Tour*, an expedition that played more than 40 shows in the U.S., 56 gigs in Europe, 24 shows throughout Oceania, and a handful of shows in Asia. The group were now veterans of the touring experience—despite having yet to release an album, be signed to a record label, or celebrate their nineteenth birthdays! This was unprecedented. The 5SOS experience was a unique one: fame on the Internet had given them an opportunity to perform their music all over the planet, before they had even had a chance to record any of their new songs. But this baptism of fire is what has kept the band on their toes.

"Us touring is kind of like rehearsal," Calum has said of this chaotic time, "but I guess you can't really rehearse for stadiums. You have to just be thrown into the deep end and go from there." 2013 became a turning point for the boys—it helped them transform into better musicians and got them used to screaming fans from an early date. As Ash said in 2013, "You know, we've not released much of our music, but the kids didn't care, they seemed to know every word. I guess they'd been watching live videos on YouTube, finding the lyrics over all the screaming girls. It's incredible!"

With the *Take Me Home Tour* complete in November 2013, 5SOS needed some time off to give their ears a break from all the screaming fans. But instead of putting their feet up, they went straight back to work. In the same month as the first 1D tour ended, the band made their dreams come true—they signed a record deal with Capitol Records and set to work writing and recording their debut album. They had the fans. They had the songs. They had their dream record deal. All they needed now was a hit track that would rocket them to the top of the charts. 2014 was just around the corner, and as it turned out, it was the year that put 5SOS on the map—literally. They were out on tour again, but this time they had a not-so-secret weapon...

BEFORE THEY BECAME GLOBAL MEGA-STARS, 5SOS PLAY A ONE DIRECTION SUPPORT SHOW IN BIRMINGHAM, U.K. IN 2013. LOOK HOW YOUNG THEY SEEM COMPARED TO TODAY!

IN THE U.K., 5SOS'S FIRST ACOUSTIC SHOW, AT THE CAMDEN BARFLY, APRIL 7, 2013, SOLD OUT IN 2.3 SECONDS!

WHAT A LINE-UP! THE THREE GUITARISTS TAKE TO THE STAGE IN 2013. MIKE EVEN HAS HIS "NORMAL" HAIR COLOR—VERY RARE!

MIKE AND CAL LEAP INTO THE AIR AT THE O2 ABC, GLASGOW, AT THE START OF THEIR U.K. AND EUROPEAN TOUR.

STARS, STRIPES, AND 5SOS!

FOLLOWING THE SUCCESS OF A WORLDWIDE TOUR WITH ONE DIRECTION, 5SOS HAD STARTED THE YEAR 2014 ON A HIGH. BUT AS IT TURNED OUT, THEIR RISE TO FAME WAS ONLY JUST GETTING STARTED. AND AS FEBRUARY ROLLED AROUND, LIFE WAS ABOUT TO GET EVEN MORE "PERFECT"...

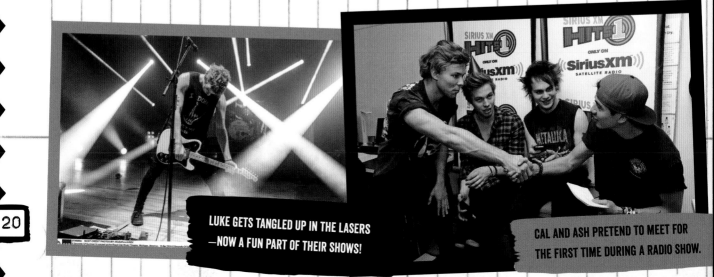

LUKE GETS TANGLED UP IN THE LASERS —NOW A FUN PART OF THEIR SHOWS!

CAL AND ASH PRETEND TO MEET FOR THE FIRST TIME DURING A RADIO SHOW.

On February 23, 2014, 5SOS released their major breakout single, "She Looks So Perfect." It shot to Number 1 in Australia and the U.K., and broke the Top 20 in the U.S.— an unbelievable achievement considering that they had signed their own record deal only two months prior.

With a Number 1 song to their name, 5SOS jumped on a plane—many planes, in fact—and went on their 5 Countries 5 Days European Tour, where they played five shows to five sold-out crowds in Sweden, Germany, France, Italy, and Spain. Fans waited for them outside radio show appearances, outside the gig venues, and at the airport—5SOS-mania had now spread throughout Europe like wildfire!

In April 2014—and now members of the hottest live band on the planet—Ash, Cal, Luke, and Mike took things to a whole new level: they set off on a mini, month-long U.S. extravaganza, called the Stars, Stripes, and Maple Syrup Tour. With many U.S. fans still only aware of 5SOS as One Direction's support act, it was clear that 5SOS wanted to prove they were a live band with a strong desire to be taken seriously. Playing ten shows across the U.S., from San Francisco to Los Angeles, Dallas to Chicago, Toronto to New York, the band's first ever North American headline tour was an unqualified success. It was also a brave thing to do, showing music journalists that they were a group who wanted to be taken as genuine musicians and to step outside of One Direction's "boy band" shadow.

"With the 5 Seconds of Summer live experience you should be expecting a rock show, guitar solos, and high energy!" Ash exclaimed proudly while on the SASAMP Tour in the U.S. "We love making a crowd move and creating a big energy throughout the show and we hope to leave an impression so you leave wanting more!" That's exactly what they did—and then some! Tickets for 2015's Rocks Out With Your Socks Out Tour sold out in minutes. With America devoured, 5SOS were within arm's reach of world domination. But before that, the group decided to go back to the place where all their success had begun for one last tour to see the year out. This was a place they had not seen in more than twelve months, a place where their fans had desperately missed them, a place that they called home. It was time to go and rock the socks off of Australia.

THE GUYS ATTEND A PHOTO SHOOT AT MONDADORI PIAZZA DUOMO IN MILAN, ITALY, JUNE 2014. MIKE'S GONE GREEN!

LUKE LOOKS SO PERFECT STANDING THERE IN HIS AMERICAN APPAREL SKINNY JEANS!

21

GETTING FIRED UP BACKSTAGE AT THE 2014 AMERICAN MUSIC AWARDS IN LOS ANGELES, ABOUT TO PLAY IN FRONT OF HUNDREDS OF THEIR MUSICAL HEROES—EEK!

THE BAND'S LIVE SHOW IS AN AUDIO AND VISUAL FEAST INCLUDING LASERS, DRY ICE, HUGE SCREENS, AND FIREWORKS!

IN 2014, 5SOS TRAVELED ALL OVER THE PLANET IN SUPPORT OF THEIR OWN HUGE TOURS. NEXT STOP... MARS!

NO PLACE LIKE HOME

5SOS'S FIFTH HEADLINE TOUR, AND THEIR SEVENTH TOUR OVERALL, SAW THEM RETURN HOME TO AUSTRALIA... AND BE WELCOMED BACK LIKE ACTION HEROES! WITH LOCAL SUPPORT ACTS LITTLE SEA AND MIKE DIGNAM, THE BAND PERFORMED SEVEN SHOWS AND GAVE THEIR UNCONDITIONAL LOVE AND THANKS TO THEIR FIRST FANS AT HOME WHO MADE ALL THEIR DREAMS COME TRUE.

Beginning at Sydney's Enmore Theatre on April 30, 2014, 5SOS's *There's No Place Like Home Tour* was as triumphant as it was emotional for the four boys from Sydney. Gigs in Adelaide, Melbourne's Palais Theatre, Brisbane, and Perth saw 5 Seconds of Summer rock Australia's winter time with style!

The band's arrival in Australia at Sydney, Adelaide, and Brisbane airports saw hundreds of fans cause chaos with security, and the guys hit the local headlines at each of the cities where the tour played. Their Aussie fans, it seemed, were determined to show their foreign fans they were still the loudest! "Our Aussie fans definitely started us off," Ashton said as a way of thanking their biggest and liveliest supporters. "They're incredible to us and they're the reason we began."

As the band prepares to go on their *Rock Out With Their Socks Out Tour* in the Summer of 2015—a tour that is guaranteed to be bigger and better than any tour on the planet—5SOS has expressed a desire to have more "dudes" in their audience, as well as hopefully garner a more mature response from their fans. "As our fans grow up, so will our music," said Mike at the end of this 2014 tour. "I think it's just a matter of time, we are definitely not going anymore pop than we have now. Some of our fans are very young. If you come to a 5SOS show and you are really young, stay at the back and wear earplugs!" 5SOS live and loud in the future—you have all been warned!

During the performance of "Disconnected," which Luke thinks is "probably the best song we've ever written," he asks the thousands of fans to "put their mobile phones away, because this song is about living in the moment." It's a tender little scene during what turned out to be an emotional tour, which has seen the band reconnect with their Australian fans, friends, and family.

LIVE, TONIGHT, SOLD OUT

PROOF, WERE IT NEEDED, THAT 5SOS IS A TRULY INSPIRING LIVE BAND IS THE FACT THAT SIX MONTHS AFTER THE DEBUT ALBUM PUNCHED A MASSIVE HOLE IN THE CHARTS, THEY RELEASED THEIR FIRST LIVE ALBUM, *LIVESOS*.

BACKSTAGE STRETCHES FOR DRUMMER ASH AT THE 2014 IHEARTRADIO MUSIC FESTIVAL IN LAS VEGAS.

It's very rare that young bands choose to release live albums so soon in their career, especially after having just released one album, and especially if you are considered to be a "boy band." But so strong are 5SOS as a live band—and so important is it to them to be taken seriously as an authentic group —that they released a live album of their own material to their fans as a declaration of intent about their entire existence: WE ARE A LIVE BAND.

The release of 5SOS's *LiveSOS* also proves that when it comes to their own music, Luke, Ash, Cal, and Mike are the only people in charge. "I always want to know that we're the ones making the choices. We're the ones who decide what we do. When we see negative comments in the press, they genuinely get us down, we want our fans to understand what decisions we make." Well said, Ashton! His bandmate, Luke agrees: "We get the boyband tag a lot, we don't try and fight it, but it doesn't really fit. We want to be a pop rock band with a punk edge!"

When on tour with One Direction, they may be mercilessly (but affectionately) labeled The Emos by Harry Styles, but 5SOS's music cannot be judged so quickly. Like their hearts,

LIVESOS TRACK LISTING

WHICH SONG IS YOUR FAVORITE?

"18"

"Out Of My Limit"

"Disconnected"—"probably the best song we've ever written" says Luke!

"Amnesia"

"Beside You"

"Everything I Didn't Say"

"Long Way Home"

"Heartache On The Big Screen"

"American Idiot"—the Green Day song!

"Teenage Dream"—the Katy Perry song!

"Good Girls"

"What I Like About You"

"End Up Here"

"She Looks So Perfect"

they wear their influences on their T-shirt sleeves, and bands such as Good Charlotte, Nirvana, Green Day, Yellowcard, and Metallica have all been name-checked in interviews before. As Calum says, "As long as we're making the music we want to make, what people call us doesn't matter."

LiveSOS was announced on November 22, 2014, and the album includes 15 live performances of songs from the debut album and previously released EPs. With the release of the album on December 15, 2014, an early Christmas present for all their fans to celebrate the end of a year that had seen them become the biggest band in the world, 5SOS released a statement that read like the band's de facto declaration of intent for the future: "Playing live has been something we have been the most passionate about from the beginning. All we want is for our fans to come to the shows, rock out, and have one of the best times they've ever experienced. Also, when a room is full of you guys from all different walks of life, you can let it go when you come to the shows and be free to be yourself. Our Live Album has 15 tracks recorded in different venues around the world! Anyways we love you, this is us live... You rule!"

ASH TWEETS A SNAP OF CAL LOOKING COOL BACKSTAGE AT THE AMERICAN MUSIC AWARDS 2014, LOS ANGELES.

SETLIST 2015

ROCK OUT WITH SOCKS OUT TOUR

"I've Got This Friend"
"Out of My Limit"
"Heartbreak Girl"
"Voodoo Doll"
"Don't Stop"
"Disconnected"
"Amnesia"
"Beside You"
"Long Way Home"
"Rejects"
"Heartache on the Big Screen"
"Wrapped Around Your Finger"
"Everything I Didn't Say"
"American Idiot"
"Bad Dreams"
"She Looks So Perfect"
"Good Girls"
"What I Like About You"

DO YOU HAVE YOUR TICKETS TO SEE THE BAND THIS YEAR? BETTER GET THEM QUICK BEFORE THEY ALL SELL OUT. DON'T WORRY IF YOU HAVEN'T—THEY'LL BE BACK!

APPEARING ON THE LONGEST RUNNING TALK SHOW ON AMERICAN TV—*THE TONIGHT SHOW* WITH JIMMY FALLON!

5SOS TAKE OVER DOWNTOWN NEW YORK CITY FOR THEIR APPEARANCE ON THE MOST WATCHED MORNING TV SHOW IN AMERICA—*THE TODAY SHOW*—TO AN AUDIENCE OF MILLIONS!

TV STARS

IN THE TWENTY-FIRST CENTURY, PERFORMING LIVE USUALLY MEANS PLAYING IN FRONT OF THOUSANDS OF PEOPLE IN THE AUDIENCE, AS WELL AS FOR MILLIONS OF PEOPLE WATCHING AT HOME, WHO ARE EITHER STREAMING THE GIG, WATCHING IT ON YOUTUBE, OR FILMING IT ON THEIR SMART PHONE AND SHOWING IT TO THEIR FRIENDS. THANKFULLY, 5SOS ARE AS GOOD TO LOOK AT AS THEY ARE TO SING ALONG TO, SO THEY DON'T MIND WHO'S WATCHING...

From MTV Music Award ceremonies to late night talk show appearances, such as America's most watched program *Late Night With Jimmy Fallon*, as well as appearing on *Google's Hangout* and a multitude of other online TV channels, 5SOS rock up and rock out in order to promote their music to audiences in different countries and different languages, all over the world. But sometimes appearing on TV shows can become quite tiresome for the band. As musicians, they don't always feel comfortable talking about themselves in order to sell their music. More often than not, they like their music to speak for itself. As Ash so eloquently put it, in an interview in 2014, "To be in a band that wanted to conquer the world you had to be louder than life, you had to be a character. We didn't like that. We felt a bit awkward talking to people." As many musicians discover, constantly being on TV and promoting yourself can be a hard task—especially after a long flight or a big show the night before. We must remember that before all the glory, the boys were just four teenagers who had never expected to experience such intense fame. "We don't think anybody's really properly ready for it," Luke

said, talking about the scrutiny of performing live on TV in front of thousands of people. "It's certainly a ride! We've been thrown in the deep end a lot, but it's all part of it. I've learned how to make 10,000 or even 70,000 people feel that they're part of it. It's not just playing the songs and playing them perfectly. You've got to be this massive entity on stage, and just bring people in and make them have a good time."

The band's most high-profile TV appearance —and live performance—to date came in November 2014, when fans of the band led a social media campaign to get the band on the iconic *The Ellen DeGeneres Show*—a program that has more than five million daily viewers. During the show, Ellen asked fans to perform an interview segment with the boys called "5 Seconds With 5 Seconds of Summer." Various fans of the band were given five seconds in which they could ask the band whatever questions they liked. For some reason, all four of the the boys ended up with their pants down by their ankles! After chatting with the friendly TV host and Oscar host, the group performed "Good Girls" live on the show to the small, but adoring, crowd of loud fans.

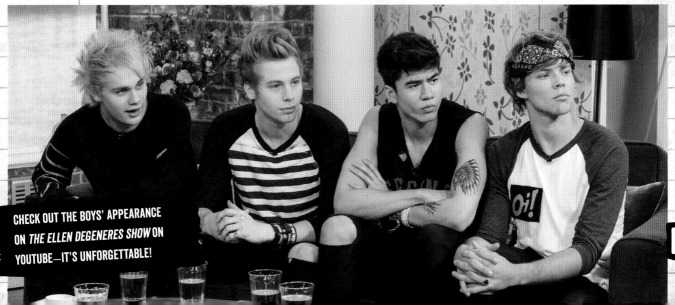

CHECK OUT THE BOYS' APPEARANCE ON *THE ELLEN DEGENERES SHOW* ON YOUTUBE—IT'S UNFORGETTABLE!

FOR THE RELEASE OF THEIR SECOND
MAJOR SINGLE, "DON'T STOP," THE BAND
GO TO GREAT HEIGHTS TO GET IT HEARD!

BE KIND REWIND

WHEN NOT TOURING, PERFORMING LIVE, OR RECORDING NEW MATERIAL IN THE STUDIO, 5SOS CAN USUALLY BE SEEN HAVING FUN IN THEIR WILD AND AWESOME MUSIC VIDEOS. FROM THE SUPERHERO SILLINESS OF "DON'T STOP" TO THE STRIPPED DOWN NAUGHTINESS OF "SHE LOOKS SO PERFECT," THE BOMBASTIC HEAVINESS OF "WHAT I LIKE ABOUT YOU" OR THE HOMEMADE CLUB PERFORMANCE OF "OUT OF MY LIMIT," THE MEGA-VIDEOS THAT 5SOS MAKE FOR THEIR FANS ARE A FEAST FOR THEIR EARS AND THEIR EYES!

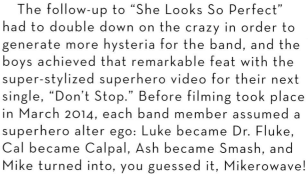

Luke once said that, "We like our shows to be a big party vibe, y'know? We want it to be an amazing experience. We want a show that fans can get involved in." Well, it looks like they've taken that attitude and applied it to their music videos, too! With more than 120 million views on YouTube so far —by far their most popular—the promo clip to "She Looks So Perfect" caused a storm when it first dropped on the Internet in February 2014. It instantly became a fan favorite and their support meant that it was proclaimed as one of the best international videos of the year!

"I think we've never wanted anything more than for people to get nude in a video of ours!" Ash said at the time of the clip's release. "The director, Frank Borin, came to us with the idea and we're like, 'That's absolutely perfect.' He's like, 'Yeah, the song should put people in a craze and make them want to take their clothes off.' And I was like, 'Sounds good.'" The video sent Twitter and Facebook into meltdown, with fans sharing this wacky new video from "this cute Aussie boy band."

The follow-up to "She Looks So Perfect" had to double down on the crazy in order to generate more hysteria for the band, and the boys achieved that remarkable feat with the super-stylized superhero video for their next single, "Don't Stop." Before filming took place in March 2014, each band member assumed a superhero alter ego: Luke became Dr. Fluke, Cal became Calpal, Ash became Smash, and Mike turned into, you guessed it, Mikerowave!

With currently more than 11 million views on YouTube, the song certainly helped to generate more male fans for the band. To promote the video and the song in July 2014, the boys went one step further than just your average bands; they decided to rappel down London's Senate House—a building 210 feet (64 meters) high!—in their superhero costumes, while giant pictures of them were projected onto the side of the building for the whole of London to see! It was a stunt of epic proportions and helped propel the song to the Top 10 in many countries, selling almost 200,000 copies in the U.K.

So, what's your favorite 5SOS music video?

LIVE AND ONLINE

AS EVERYBODY KNOWS, 5SOS'S CLOSE RELATIONSHIP WITH THEIR FANS IS THE MOST IMPORTANT THING TO THEM. OVER THE PAST FOUR YEARS, THAT RELATIONSHIP HAS BLOSSOMED BEAUTIFULLY, LARGELY DUE TO THE BAND'S BRILLIANT USE OF SOCIAL MEDIA SITES SUCH AS FACEBOOK, TWITTER, AND INSTAGRAM, AS WELL AS THEIR OWN *WWW.5SOS.COM* WEBSITE.

Hello 5SOS Fam! With the band rolling and LOL-ing around the world on their *Rock Out With Your Socks Out Tour* in 2015, and with further headline tours and a new album due later in the year, it seems it will be a long time before the boys settle down in one place. So, if you want to keep up to date with them and where they are when they are on tour, the best thing to do is to follow them online at Twitter, Facebook, or Instagram. That way you can keep in touch with them—no matter where they are!

Social media has been super-important for the band since their very first days, which was singled out, in 2014, when the group was nominated for a Shorty Award for Best Use of Social Media. Toward the end of 2014, the boys were even the subject of a social media campaign when millions of the band's U.S. fans all joined together to form the "Get 5 Seconds of Summer on Ellen" campaign, an online event that sought to get the band to perform on *The Ellen DeGeneres Show*—one of the U.S.'s most watched shows, and a place where only the biggest celebrities are allowed to go! The band's combined 20 million online followers meant that it wasn't long before the talk show host Ellen DeGeneres heard what was going on and immediately called the band to perform on her show, as well as take part in a very candid and funny interview. So, what are we all waiting for? Let's all join forces with our friends and get 5SOS to come to our

hometowns and perform—all it takes is one person to get it going!

With online being the place to be to share performance photos, videos, and chat directly with The 5SOS Fam, it's no wonder that each member of the band has more than five million followers. "It would be much harder to share with our fans without Facebook and Twitter for sure," Luke has said. "I think fans have changed and how they support musicians has changed. People want to know about you and who you are; without the ways to speak to them, I really don't think we would be where we are today." Ashton agrees: "Social media for us has been huge for connecting with the fans. It's also been important for us to make sure our fans know exactly who we are, where we are, and what we're doing."

"It's incredible that people are banging on the windows. As a musician, that's something that you dream of," said Ashton in 2014. The band's fans have been knocking on their windows, online, with each member posting pictures, tweets, and updates several times a day. Check out their incredible 5SOSelfies!

"We're not really from much, so to have this opportunity, it all comes back to our fanbase. We've heard lots on Twitter and we work a lot on social media because that's where we started really, but it's just so good to see the fans on tour. It would be much harder to share with our fans without Facebook and Twitter for sure!" said Calum to Fuse Online in 2014.

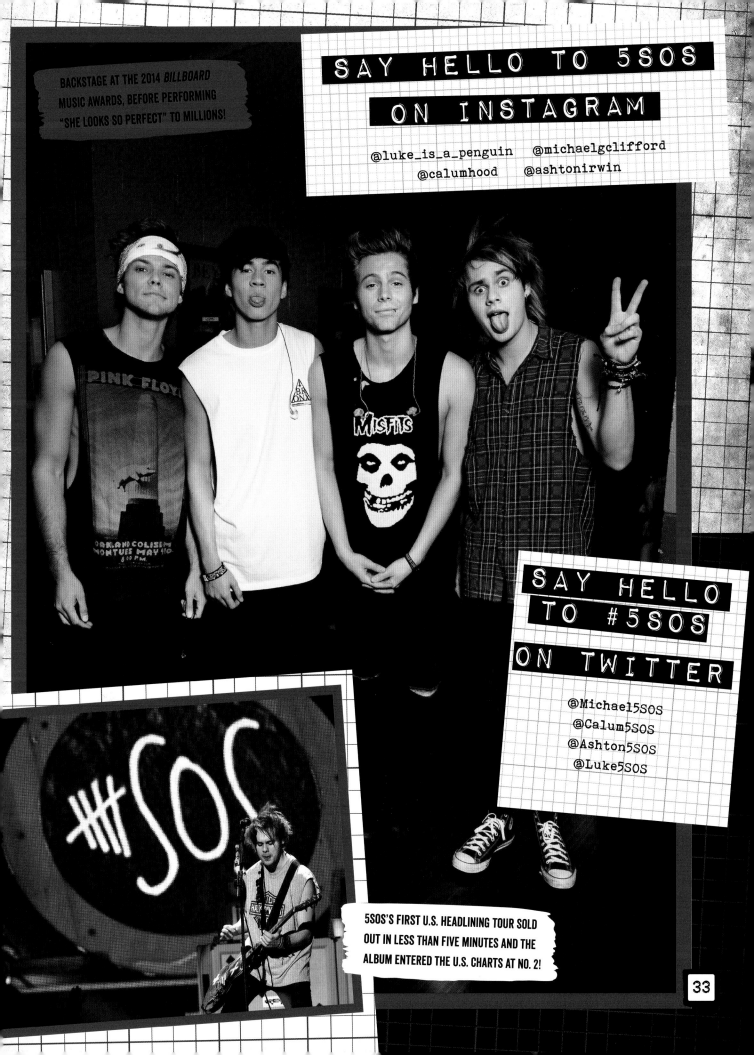

BACKSTAGE AT THE 2014 *BILLBOARD* MUSIC AWARDS, BEFORE PERFORMING "SHE LOOKS SO PERFECT" TO MILLIONS!

SAY HELLO TO 5SOS ON INSTAGRAM

@luke_is_a_penguin   @michaelgclifford
@calumhood   @ashtonirwin

SAY HELLO TO #5SOS ON TWITTER

@Michael5SOS
@Calum5SOS
@Ashton5SOS
@Luke5SOS

5SOS'S FIRST U.S. HEADLINING TOUR SOLD OUT IN LESS THAN FIVE MINUTES AND THE ALBUM ENTERED THE U.S. CHARTS AT NO. 2!

ACCESS ALL AREAS

5 SECONDS OF SUMMER LIKES TO HAVE FUN. ANYONE WHO KNOWS ANYTHING ABOUT THE BAND KNOWS THAT WHEN MIKE, CAL, LUKE, AND ASH ARE IN THE SAME ROOM TOGETHER EVERYTHING, AND ANYTHING, IS POSSIBLE...

Since the band first performed together in 2011, and practiced with each other in their parents' garages, right through to organizing, and performing, their tours, and to managing all their own social media and relationships with their fans (and even setting up and running their own record label), 5SOS has always taken their music very seriously. The boys like to be in control of everything they do because they want to have success on their own terms. But when it comes to taking time off, or enjoying themselves off-duty from their hectic touring and publicity schedules, the boys take having fun seriously, too—and

like to take it to the next level! Including getting naked every now and again, which seems to be the band's favorite thing to do when on tour!

"When we first got our tour bus in America," Luke revealed in an interview in 2014, "I remember in the first half an hour of meeting the tour bus driver he saw me naked! I thought that was kind of weird. I was running up and down the tour bus without any clothes on! It was funny!" There was also the infamous incident of when, on the *Where We Are Tour* in 2014, Mike saw Harry Styles in the buff! "All I remember is Harry coming into our room, stealing all our fruit, throwing fruit at us, tipping our tables over and running away naked," Mike said. "It was traumatizing!" Luke also recalls a special moment he and Calum shared—quite literally with the world. "Once when we lived in London, I went downstairs and Calum was making a cup of tea naked, so I took a photo. Calum's butt is everywhere now!"

But their pranks on tour don't just stop at being naked; they like to have fun fully clothed, too. In December 2014, winding down toward the end of a very busy year, the boys decided to disguise their handsome looks and dress up as grandmas and grandpas to attend the Jingle Ball in Washington D.C.—their final live show of the year. Showing off their playful side, the boys descended on America's political capital looking like elderly people. "We wanted to mix it up," Ash exclaimed, "this is the last radio show of the year and we wanted to do something fun, so we dressed up." Luke and Mike held little purses, Ash and Cal wore thick gray mustaches, and they definitely looked the part, even though the Jingle Ball wasn't formal. Ash even admitted they were being deliberately wacky just to spice the festive show up a little bit more: "You may be wondering why we're doing this and the answer is... we don't know!" After the live performance, the band tweeted a photo (see opposite page!) with the caption, "Today was great—weird and wonderful, lol xx."

MIKE AND LUKE ARE REAL-LIFE GUITAR HEROES AND CAN OFTEN BE SEEN GUITAR DUELLING ONSTAGE!

THE BAND SPENDS A DAY AT THE RACES AT AINTREE RACECOURSE, LIVERPOOL. ASH WENT DRESSED AS A BANANA, NATURALLY!

"WE TRY TO GET A FRESH PUPPY-IT HAS TO BE WARM AND CUDDLY." -CALUM, ON THE BAND'S BACKSTAGE TOUR REQUESTS

LUKE-LIVE

AS THE YOUNGEST OF THE BAND, LUKE HEMMINGS MAY BE THE LEADER OF THE BAND (AND THE CUTEST), BUT DON'T LET HIS STRAIGHT-UP HAIR FOOL YOU—THIS HUNKY HEARTTHROB IS HERE TO PARTY HARD AND WRITE SOME AWESOMELY POWERFUL POP-PUNK SONGS, TOO!

Luke Hemmings was always going to be a famous pop icon. Born on July 16, 1996, the blond, handsome lead singer of 5SOS, with his iconic lip ring, has been on a quest to perform live and loud to as many people as possible ever since he was a young boy. At the age of 13, Luke set up his very own YouTube account name "Hemmo1996" and got himself to work learning the chords and lyrics to modern pop and rock hits. He was first inspired to become a singer and songwriter after watching Good Charlotte perform in Sydney at the Big top Luna Park in 2010.

The first video Luke uploaded to the site was the rather aptly named, "Please Don't Go" by Mike Posner. Luke hasn't left YouTube since, though his videos have changed a lot.

While on tour, Luke has a list of requests of items that he likes to have in the band's dressing room, known as a tour rider. 5SOS, of course, don't take theirs seriously at all! On his tour rider, Luke asks for a puppy, his bandmates, his toothbrush, socks, Selena Gomez, and a happy gorilla! It's unknown how many of these items he actually receives, but it is a valuable insight into the singer's mind!

LUKE TAKES A SHOWER ONSTAGE AT THE IHEART RADIO SHOW IN 2014.

When it comes to being out front onstage, rocking thousands of fans every night, it is Luke who leaps the highest from the center of the stage and—come the end of the show—is covered in sweat and has a huge smile. For Luke, there is no greater thrill than putting on a good performance for their adoring fans who have traveled from far and wide.

THE YOUNGEST MEMBER OF THE BAND.
IS LUKE THE CUTEST MEMBER OF 5SOS?
OR IS IT CAL? OR MIKE? OR ASH?

MIKE - LIVE

5SOS'S MOST MUSICALLY-MINDED MEMBER WHO WANTS THE GROUP
TO BE TAKEN SERIOUSLY, IS ALSO THE ONE WHO LOVES TO JOKE
AROUND, CONSTANTLY STICKING HIS TONGUE OUT WHEN HAVING HIS
PICTURE TAKEN, AND *ALWAYS* HAVING SOMETHING FUNNY TO SAY...

IS MIKE THE WILD ONE, AS CAL CLAIMS?
HE'S CERTAINLY THE JOKER OF THE BAND!

MIKE DELIGHTS HIS BANDMATES AFTER WINNING NEW ARTIST OF THE YEAR AT THE 2014 AMERICAN MUSIC AWARDS.

Born on November 20, 1995, Michael Clifford is the member responsible for getting the band together. The band's clown, he's a renowned backstage FIFA player and gamer, and the owner of the wackiest, most brightly colored hair to be seen in a pop band since Matt from Busted! With four tattoos and an eye piercing, Mike is also the most experimental when it comes to trying out edgy new looks, especially with his one-of-a-kind "reverse skunk" hairstyle. "I was just looking for colors that I haven't had yet," Mike revealed about how he chooses his hair color. Michael might be known as the "wild one" of the group, according to Calum (though Michael thinks "Calum is the weirdest person in the band, but he refuses to admit it!"), but when it comes to how the band is perceived, as songwriters and performers, it is Michael who is the most vocal and level-headed—even if he did want to call the band The Powerpuff Blokes when they first started rehearsing in his parents' garage!

DID YOU KNOW MICHAEL WAS VOTED CELEBRITY TWEETER OF THE YEAR BY SUGARSCAPE MAGAZINE?

CAL-LIVE

BEING A BASSIST IN A POP-PUNK GROUP IS USUALLY THE HARDEST JOB OF ANY MEMBER, BUT CALUM HOOD MAKES IT LOOK EASY AND SUPER COOL! PROVIDING THE BAND WITH THUNDERING BASSLINES AND AN ENERGETIC LIVE SPIRIT—AND FOREVER JUMPING UP AND DOWN!— OUR CAL IS A MIGHTY KIWI DEMON...

"I don't know how it happened that Calum got in the band. No one officially asked Calum to join!" said Michael who, to this day, still teases Calum about the day that the bassist joined 5SOS. "He was just friends with us and assumed he was in the band!"

No matter how he joined, Calum Hood, born on January 25, 1995, is 5SOS's ferocious bass player. A multi-talented instrumentalist, he is also the only member of a pop band in modern history to be part Kiwi and part Scottish!

It was while at Norwest Christian College, that Calum, along with Mike, first saw Luke's YouTube videos and believed he had something special about him, in particular the singer's magical voice. At school, Calum was more shy than Luke and Mike, and on the constant lookout for an outlet for his creative musical talents; he saw performing live with Luke and Mike as a way to gain some much-needed confidence. "We were just really into music," Calum revealed of the time the band first met, "and every lunch we'd be inside playing guitars and jamming out, so not much 'social action' was happening!" he said. "I was just very reserved. The band's helped me have a voice."

From cute and cuddly, to tall and hairy— and now undeniably cool—Calum has done a lot of growing up since becoming a world famous international rock star. But he still has moments of embarrassment when performing live, moments that make him think of being back at school. As he recalls: "I once split my pants from my crotch to my knee on stage,

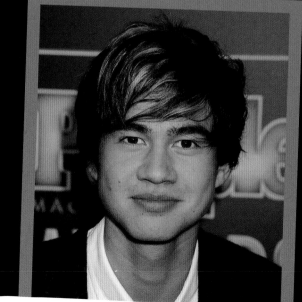

MUSIC MAD CALUM WROTE "DON'T STOP" WITH LUKE FOR THEIR DEBUT ALBUM.

40

> "LUKE WOULD BE THE SHY ONE, ASHTON IS THE TALKER AND THE FUNNY ONE, MICHAEL IS THE WILD ONE... AND I'M JUST THE CHILL DUDE."
> —CALUM

so I had to go backstage while the stage was dark and duct tape my leg, but still be playing at the same time!" he said, remembering the moment while the band was on the U.S. leg of their *Stars and Stripes and Maple Syrup Tour*. "That was kind of hard to do and it was pretty embarrassing. In the end, I just had to announce it to the crowd to make it less embarrassing!" Thankfully, Calum had his bandmates by his side to help him through.

"I think the three best things about being in 5SOS is being with your best friends that you grew up with, doing the thing you love. We're all really good friends. I couldn't imagine being in a band with people I didn't like," Calum said, "and they're my brothers now." Calum's one request on his backstage tour rider is "Just a hug." Let's hope he got a few after that infamous pant-ripping show!

CAL ROCKS OUT WITH HIS TONGUE OUT AT KIIS-FM'S JINGLE BALL, DECEMBER 5, 2014 IN LOS ANGELES.

ASH - LIVE

WHAT'S SMOKIN' HOT AND ON FIRE? ASH! ASHTON FLETCHER IRWIN IS THE OLDEST MEMBER OF 5SOS AND THE ONE PERSON RESPONSIBLE FOR KEEPING THE REST OF THE GUYS ON TIME—IF ONLY ON STAGE! WITH HIS NOW-ICONIC BANDANA, CUTE SMILE, AND LOVE OF CLASSIC ROCK, ASH IS DEFINITELY THE "TALKER" OF THE GROUP, AS WELL AS THE MEMBER MOST HOTLY-TIPPED TO BECOME EVERYONE'S FAVORITE CELEBRITY OF THE NEAR-FUTURE.

TIMEKEEPER ASH BEATS THE SKINS AND POWERS THE BAND'S UPBEAT SONGS— HE IS AN AMAZING DRUMMER!

"In 2011 I was working in a video shop," Ashton, born in 1994, recalls of the time when Luke, Cal, and Mike first started forming 5SOS during Math classes at Norwest Christian College. By night, Ash was a drummer for the band Swallow the Goldfish. "I was a drummer in the local area, and these boys needed a drummer for their first gig and so I went and played with them and it just felt really right on stage... and so I joined the band that day." Legend has it that after the band's first show at a local pub, The Annandale Hotel, Cal wanted to thank Ashton for helping the guys out when they

needed a drummer at the last minute, so he bent "down on one knee and proposed to Ashton to be in the band." ("There's a photo of this moment," Luke reckons!) Ashton said yes... and the rest is soon pop, punk, and rock history! Ash is the oldest and most mature, and when he first joined the band he disliked their rehearsals because the other members used to "mess around too much" and never concentrated on learning to get through a whole song without messing up. But, as he said a few years later, this was all part of the fun of being in a band and learning how to play together. "You have to suck at the

TAKING INSPIRATION FROM HIS HEROES—DAVE GROHL AND TRE COOL—ASH LOOKS EVERY PART THE ICONIC ROCK DRUMMER!

"I'D BEEN PLAYING MY STEPDAD'S DRUMS AT HOME IN THE GARAGE AND ONE DAY HE ASKED ME ON STAGE TO PLAY THE SONG "SWEET HOME ALABAMA" BY LYNYRD SKYNYRD. I GOT TO PERFORM IN FRONT OF A CROWD OF 100 PEOPLE AND IT WAS THE GREATEST THING EVER. THAT SPURRED ON MY DESIRE TO PERFORM FOR PEOPLE."—ASH

beginning and you have to have crap for instruments and not be able to afford stuff and work from the bottom for the band to grow. I guess we always wanted to be a hard working rock band," he reflected in 2013. "We always looked up to bands like Green Day, and it was really important to us to stand up for what we wanted to be as a band." A point that, Ashton says, is made clear in the drummer's signature bandana—he is never pictured on stage without it! It's a style that is more than just a fashion statement. "I really like what my bandana represents," Ashton revealed, finally explaining why he wears them. "It's more than just a fashion thing to me. It represents my inspirations. I look up to a lot of old-school drummers from the 70s, 80s, and 90s. They used to wear bandanas to signify they were rock!" Well, now you know!

DURING THEIR SET'S SLOWER SONGS, ASH PLAYS THE BONGOS OR TAPS A RHYTHM ON A BOX, AND SOMETIMES EVEN PLAYS BASS!

BACKSTAGE ON HOME SOIL, MARTIN PLACE, MAY 15, 2014, SYDNEY.

THE BAND HAS WON COUNTLESS AWARDS, FROM FAVORITE BREAKOUT ARTIST TO AUSSIES' FAVE HOT NEW TALENT!

WINNING!

WE'VE KNOWN FOREVER THAT 5SOS ARE WINNERS, BUT EVER SINCE 5SOS COMPLETED THEIR FIRST HEADLINE TOUR, AND RELEASED THEIR DEBUT SINGLE "OUT OF MY LIMIT," THE BAND HAS BEEN PICKING UP AWARDS FOR BEING AWESOME AT GLITZY CEREMONIES ALL OVER THE WORLD.

In June 2014—seemingly against all odds—another one of 5SOS's dreams came true. They were nominated for Best International newcomer at the annual awards ceremony of the heavy metal magazine *Kerrang!*. No one in the world—in particular, the band themselves—were expecting them to win. But they did! "It is a real honor for us," Luke said of this historic win, the first time a perceived "boy band" has won a prestigious *Kerrang!* award, and especially coming so close after the band's tour with One Direction began. "All of our idols are in this magazine," Luke continued, "We can't be more grateful for this... it means a lot to us."

Despite the snobby world music press being unable to make their mind up about 5SOS (are they a boy band or a true punk group?) and the boys winning Worst Band at the trendy *NME* Awards in February 2015—a magazine that has never supported 5SOS, presumably for the members' close connection to One Direction—2013 and 2014 have been stellar years for 5SOS. They have been nominated and have won many prestigious honors and awards.

Most notably, of course, the boys collected MTV Europe's 2014 Music Award for Best Australian Act, the American Music Award for New Artist of the Year, *People*'s Choice Award for Favorite Breakout Artist and MTV Best Lyric Video Award 2014 for "Don't Stop," beating iconic American pop stars as Katy Perry, Demi Lovato, and Ariana Grande! Thanking their fans for the Moon Man award, Mike said live onstage, "It's more than any artist and band could expect," and then the boys belted out an emotional live performance of "Amnesia." This was the quartet's first ever big moment on stage at the respected,

and long-running, MTV Video Music Awards, and they now performed their song in front of some of the biggest names in the industry, including Kanye West, Beyoncé, Miley Cyrus, and Nicki Minaj. This is one of the industry's biggest nights of the year.

The greatest award highlight for the band came in 2014, when 5SOS won the mega-prestigious honor of Song Of The Year for "She Looks So Perfect" at the Australian Recording Industry Awards (ARIAs), beating nine other nominees, including Sia and Iggy Azalea. "This is the first award our parents have actually seen us get apart from participation in swimming or something, so this is very special," Calum Hood shouted while thanking the crowd. After a performance of "She Looks So Perfect." Ashton tweeted his thanks to their fans on this historic evening. "You got this for us guys... Our very first ARIA award, I'm so over the mound x," he wrote. "We're just from Sydney and it's incredible what's happened to us and we can't be thankful enough."

UNPLUGGED

IN THE BEGINNING, BEFORE ALL THE LOUD DRUMS, GUITARS, AND BASS STARTED BANGING IN OUR EARDRUMS, 5SOS WAS A MUCH QUIETER BAND. IT WAS THEIR TENDER ACOUSTIC VERSIONS OF COVERS ON YOUTUBE THAT GOT THEM RECOGNIZED, AND THEIR FIRST EVER EP RELEASE WAS CALLED UNPLUGGED—THREE SONGS THAT PERFECTLY HIGHLIGHTED HOW, WHEN THE BOYS SHOW OFF THEIR SOFTER SIDE, THEY CAN CREATE JUST AS MUCH MAGIC AS WHEN THE VOLUME IS TURNED UP ALL THE WAY.

Upon its release on June 26, 2012, the *Unplugged* EP became a fan favorite —and it is still popular. With acoustic versions of the tracks "Gotta Get Out," "I Miss You," and "Too Late," the band turned down the volume and let their more tender side be seen. "You know we're a rock band at heart," Ashton said after claiming glory at the ARIA awards in December 2014, "but I can't wait for us to develop as musicians and see what else we can do," hinting at perhaps a return to their acoustic side. Though, with Mike claiming they've "gone as poppy as they'll ever go," we suspect that 5SOS will probably go even more "metal" on the second album—wait and see!

With the release of the *Unplugged* EP, 5SOS continued to perform acoustic songs at every gig they played and during their *There's No Place Like Home, Stars, Stripes, and Maple Syrup Tour*, the group often performed "Heartbreak Girl" and "Beside You" on acoustic guitars, with Ash often playing drums on a box, and sometimes the bass guitar!

On June 30, 2013, 5SOS played their first ever U.S. headline acoustic show at Webster Hall in New York City, a show that was to see them get very up close and personal with their U.S. fans for the very first time. "NEW YORK!!! We're gonna be playing our first ever U.S. headline acoustic show there in 2 weeks on June 30!! cannot waitttttt to see you all. Lets get naked!

It is going to be EPIC X," said the band on their Facebook page.

Of course, over the years, the boys have also performed their songs acoustically at various radio shows all over the world, including the now-famous free show they performed at the Much Music backlot, Toronto, Ontario on August 1, 2014, where they had hundreds of screaming fans lined up and down the street shouting "5SOS!" and singing every lyric! For Calum, these performances are a much more intimate way to experience a live show and allows him to feel the presence of everyone in the room. In arenas, we can only really see the first three rows, which was weird for us the first time." At that point, they were so used to being able to connect with their fans in close proximity—and almost look them in the eye. Playing smaller gigs, with the instruments turned down, is a unique way to see 5SOS live, and proof that there's so much more to them than just playing loud. The acoustic performances by the band were how the band first gelled and realized they had chemistry. "We were just playing acoustic covers until we got together. When we first started, it was very raw. Just the instruments and vocals. We were just doing what we could," Mike said. The

OVER THE YEARS, THE GANG HAVE HONED THE POWER OF THEIR SONGS THROUGH PLAYING THEM ACOUSTICALLY ON RADIO SHOWS.

THOUSANDS OF FANS LINED THE STREETS TO SQUEEZE INTO A PACKED PARKING LOT TO SEE THE BAND PERFORM A FREE ACOUSTIC CONCERT, TORONTO, AUGUST 2014.

acoustic performances these days are, says Ashton, a way to address their critics and "to challenge people's thoughts about whatever they thought we were." By continuing to play acoustically, the band will constantly evolve and mature their unique sound, so that their fans can "grow with us as a band." After all, Mike, Cal, Ash, and Luke can't be leaping around on stage when they're in their thirties, can they? That said, when it comes to 5SoS, we should always expect the impossible...

DEDICATED FANS LINED UP FOR HOURS TO BE AT THE FRONT OF A RADIO PERFORMANCE, NEW YORK, JULY 2014.

ROLL CREDITS

The publishers would like to thank the following sources for their kind permission to reproduce the pictures in this book.

Key: t=Top, b=Bottom, c=Center, l=Left and r=Right.

Page 2 Kevin Mazur/Getty Images; *4-5* Ethan Miller/Getty Images; *6* Frazer Harrison/Getty Images; *7* Chris Polk/Getty Images; *8* MTV/Getty Images; *9* Christopher Polk/Getty Images; *10t* Brendon Thorne/Getty Images; *10b* WENN Ltd/Alamy; *13t* WENN Ltd/Alamy; *13b* Jeff Kravitz/Getty Images; *14* Ryan Pierse/Getty Images; *15t* Jeff Kravitz/Getty Images; *15b* Ryan Pierse/Getty Images; *16-17* Michael Hurcomb/Corbis; *18* Scott Legato/Getty Images; *19t* WENN Ltd/Alamy; *19b* WENN Ltd/Alamy; *20t* WENN Ltd/Alamy; *20bl* MediaPunch/Rex Features; *20br* Robin Marchant/Getty Images; *21t* WENN Ltd/Alamy; *21b* Myrna Suarez/Getty Images; *22t* Frazer Harrison/Getty Images; *22b* Broadimage/Rex Features; *23tl* Aflo/Rex Features; *23tc* Jeff Kravitz/Getty Images; *23tr* Michael Hurcomb/Corbis; *24* Jeff Kravitz/Getty Images; *25tl* Kevin Winter/Getty Images; *25tr* C Flanigan/Getty Images; *25br* Frazer Harrison/Getty Images; *26-27* Jason Merritt/Getty Images; *28t* © NBCUniversal/Getty Images; *28b* © NBCUniversal/Getty Images; *29* Steve Meddle/ITV/Rex Features; *30* WENN Ltd/Alamy; *31* WENN Ltd/Alamy; *33t* Larry Busacca/Getty Images; *33b* Kevin Winter/Getty Images; *34* Larry French/Getty Images; *35t* Stephen Lovekin/Getty Images; *35b* David Fisher/Rex Features; *36* Jamie McCarthy/Getty Images; *37t* Frazer Harrison/Getty Images; *37bl* David Livingston/Getty Images; *37bc* Danny Moloshok/Reuters/Corbis; *37br* Jason Merritt/Getty Images; *38t* Paul Morigi/Getty Images; *38b* Chris Polk/Getty Images; *39t* Jamie McCarthy/Getty Images; *39b* Christopher Polk/Getty Images; *40t* Scott Legato/Getty Images; *40b* Gregg DeGuire/Getty Images; *41t* Matt Jelonek/Getty Images; *41b* Christopher Polk/Getty Images; *42* Michael Hurcomb/Corbis; *43t* Graham Denholm/Getty Images; *43bl* Shirlaine Forrest/Getty Images; *43br* Fairfax Media/Getty Images; *44t* Jeff Kravitz/Getty Images; *44lc* PLP/Press Line Photos/Corbis; *44rc* Kevin Winter/Getty Images; *44lb* WENN Ltd/Alamy; *44rb* Ryan Pierse/Getty Images; *45* Mark Nolan/Getty Images; *46* Bill McCay/Getty Images; *47t* ZUMA Press, Inc./Alamy; *47b* Cindy Ord/Getty Images; *48* Maarten DeBoer/Getty Images.

Poster Jeff Kravitz/Getty Images.

Every effort has been made to acknowledge correctly and contact the source and/or copyright holder of each picture, and Carlton Books Limited apologizes for any unintentional errors or omissions, which will be corrected in future editions of this book.

THE GUYS CELEBRATE WINNING THE PRESTIGIOUS AMERICAN MUSIC AWARD FOR NEW ARTIST OF THE YEAR 2014 IN TYPICAL 5SOS STYLE!